Early
NATURAL DISASTERS
Encyclopedias

BLIZZARDS

by Samantha S. Bell

Early Encyclopedias

An Imprint of Abdo Reference
abdobooks.com

abdobooks.com

Published by Abdo Reference, a division of ABDO, PO Box 398166, Minneapolis, Minnesota 55439.

Printed in China.
102024
012025

THIS BOOK CONTAINS RECYCLED MATERIALS

Editor: Marie Pearson
Series Designers: Candice Keimig, Joshua Olson
Production Designer: Joshua Olson

Library of Congress Control Number: 2024938343

Publisher's Cataloging-in-Publication Data

Names: Bell, Samantha S., author.
Title: Blizzards / by Samantha S. Bell
Description: Minneapolis, Minnesota: Abdo Reference, 2025 | Series: Early natural disasters encyclopedias | Includes online resources and index.
Identifiers: ISBN 9781098296025 (lib. bdg.) | ISBN 9798384917021 (eBook)
Subjects: LCSH: Blizzards--Juvenile literature. | Natural disasters--Juvenile literature. | Weather--Juvenile literature. | Severe storms--Juvenile literature. | Meteorology--Juvenile literature. | Earth science--Juvenile literature. | Encyclopedias and dictionaries--Juvenile literature.
Classification: DDC 551.555--dc23

CONTENTS

INTRODUCTION

Blizzards can make it difficult to get from place to place.

What Makes a Blizzard?

Blizzards are dangerous winter snowstorms. Not every snowstorm is a blizzard. To be a blizzard, a storm must meet certain conditions.

Wind

Blizzards have strong winds. Winds must be blowing at more than 35 miles per hour (56 kmh).

These may be continuous winds. They can also be wind gusts.

What's in a Name?

The term *blizzard* originally referred to a cannon shot or musket fire. In the 1870s, a newspaper used it to refer to a snowstorm. The name stuck.

Winter months tend to be windier than summer months.

Blowing Snow

Blizzards must also have blowing snow. Strong wind lifts snow from the ground. In a blizzard, the snow rises at least eight feet (2 m) off the ground.

Visibility

A blizzard's blowing snow causes poor visibility. Visibility is how far ahead someone can see.

Blowing snow can make it difficult to see roads.

Blizzard Ingredients

There are several key ingredients needed for a storm to be called a blizzard.

Blowing snow

Winds 35 miles per hour (56 kmh) or faster

Visibility less than 0.25 miles (0.4 km)

Lasts at least three hours

In blizzards, people can see no more than 0.25 miles (0.4 km) around them. A storm can be called a blizzard only if all these conditions last for at least three hours.

The Brooks Range of Alaska is in the Arctic. Its average winter low is –67 degrees Fahrenheit (–55°C).

How Blizzards Form

Blizzards need very cold air. In the United States, cold air usually comes from the north. Blizzards also need a low-pressure system. This is an area where air pressure is lower than in the areas around it.

From Low to Equal Pressure

Air moves to make the pressure equal. The low-pressure system sucks in air. It takes in the cold air from the north. It also pulls in warm air from the south.

Low-Pressure Air Movement

A low-pressure area can cause stormy weather.

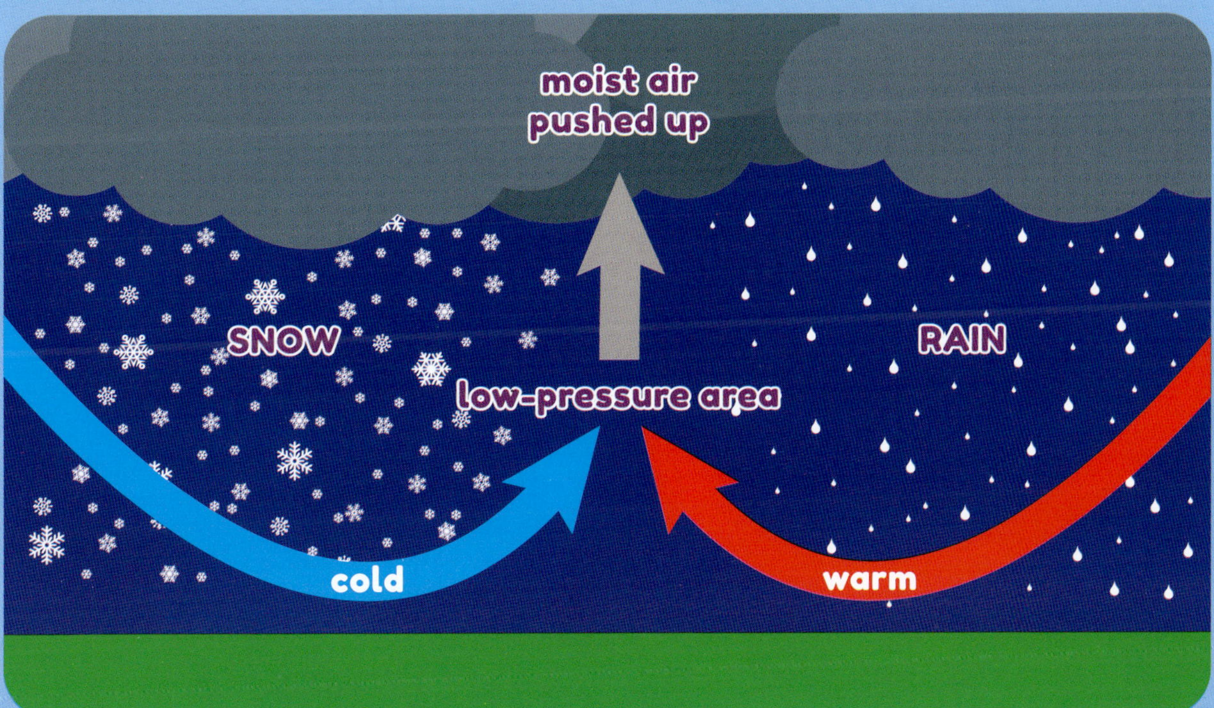

Growing Stronger

The cold air and warm air move into the low-pressure area. This creates wind. The bigger the pressure difference, the faster the air will move. The wind will be stronger.

Wind blows more steadily in places with few trees and buildings.

Blizzards can cause snow to build up on animals' fur.

Types of Blizzards

Snow does not need to fall for a blizzard to happen. There are two types of blizzards. Some have only snow on the ground. Others also have falling snow.

A Change in Direction

The winds in a low-pressure system north of the equator move in a counterclockwise direction. South of the equator, they move clockwise.

Snow can fall when the air is 32 degrees Fahrenheit (0°C) or colder.

Moisture

Snowfall blizzards need moisture in the air. This can come from winds blowing over a body of water such as a lake or an ocean. As warm winds blow, some of the water evaporates. When warm air and cold air come together, moisture in the air freezes. Snow can form.

On the Ground

Some blizzards do not have any falling snow. Instead, winds pick up snow already on the ground. These storms are called ground blizzards.

FUN FACT!

Ground blizzards can happen on a sunny day.

There can be blue sky above a ground blizzard.

Moving the Snow

Winds must travel about 12 miles per hour (19 kmh) to move snow. The snow rolls along the ground. When the wind reaches blizzard speeds of 35 miles per hour (56 kmh) or more, the snow is lifted into the air.

Blizzards cause snow to blow across roads.

Severe Blizzards

Some blizzards have very harsh conditions. These are called severe blizzards. Winds can blow at 45 miles per hour (72 kmh) or more. The temperature may be ten degrees Fahrenheit (–12°C) or lower.

Zero Visibility

Some blizzards have almost no visibility. People cannot see objects that are just a few yards away.

Blizzards can strike in West Virginia.

Seasons and Length

Blizzards are most common in winter. But they can happen at other times of the year. Some happen in spring. Others happen in the fall. Many last longer than three hours. Some last for days.

Around the World

Blizzards can happen in any place that has snowfall. Places close to the Arctic have the most blizzards. These places include Russia and northeastern Asia. Countries in northern Europe also get blizzards. Canada and the United States do too.

Tropical Blizzards

Blizzards can happen in the tropics. Storms blow across the high, cold mountaintops.

A blizzard hit Barentsburg, Norway, in May 2022.

United States

Blizzards form in most parts of the United States. Sometimes blizzards form in the Northeast. These storms are called Nor'easters. They happen when a low-pressure area moves north. The storm picks

A 2022 Nor'easter covered cars in Boston, Massachusetts, with heavy snow.

up moisture from the Atlantic Ocean. The cold temperatures turn the moisture into snow.

Midwestern Storms

The upper Midwest and Great Plains experience blizzards the most often. One reason for this is that there are few trees. Trees usually slow the wind.

The Rockies reach 10,000 to 20,000 feet (3,050 to 6,100 m) high.

Rocky Mountains

The Rocky Mountains are also known as the Rockies. They stretch from Alaska to New Mexico. Storms in the Midwest usually form near the Rockies.

Guiding Air

Cold air flows south from Canada. The Rockies block the moving air. Then the air must flow along the sides of the mountains. This causes the winds to blow faster. The cold air may mix with moisture from the Great Lakes or the Gulf of Mexico.

US Regions Map

The Great Plains and Central Lowland areas of the United States together make up a region called the Interior Lowlands or Interior Plains. This area is mostly flat and open.

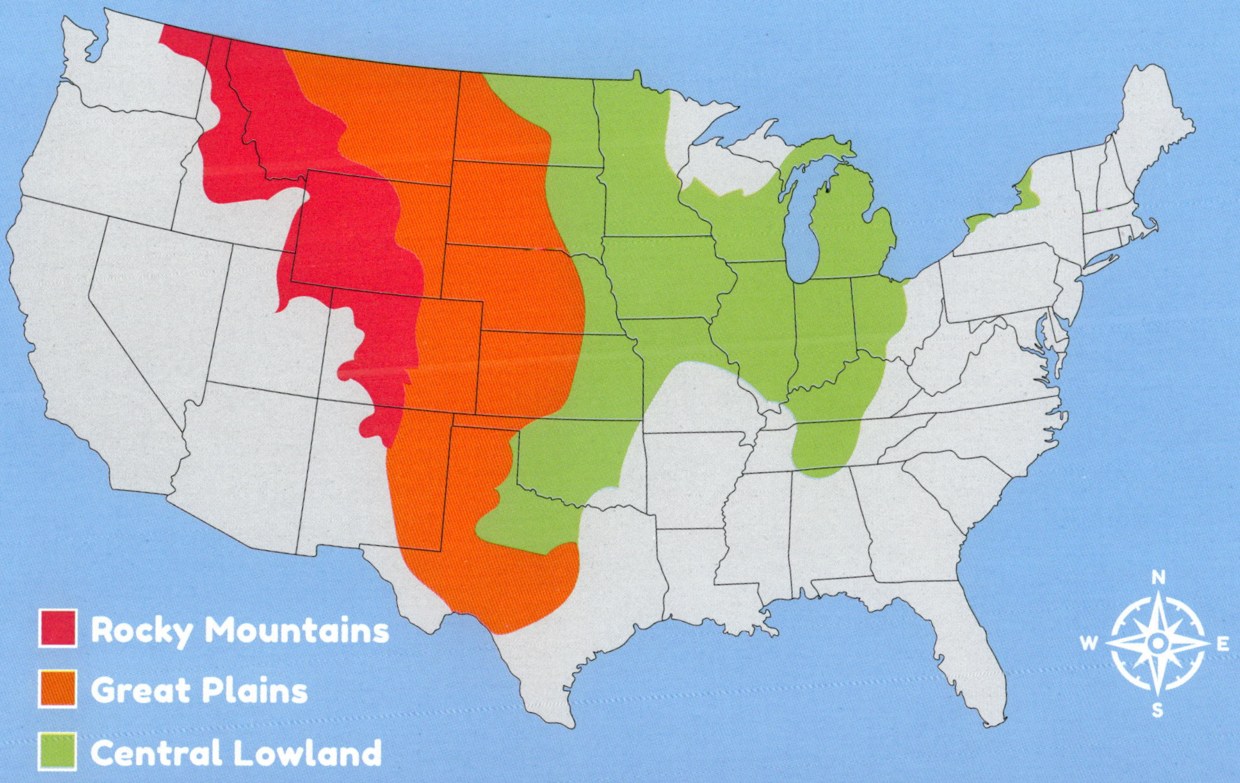

Lake-Effect Snow

Sometimes below-freezing air passes over a lake's warmer waters. Some of the water becomes moisture in the air. The moist air moves away from the lake. The air cools. This makes snow.

Making Lake-Effect Snow

Lake-effect snow pulls in moisture from a lake, creating a lot of snow.

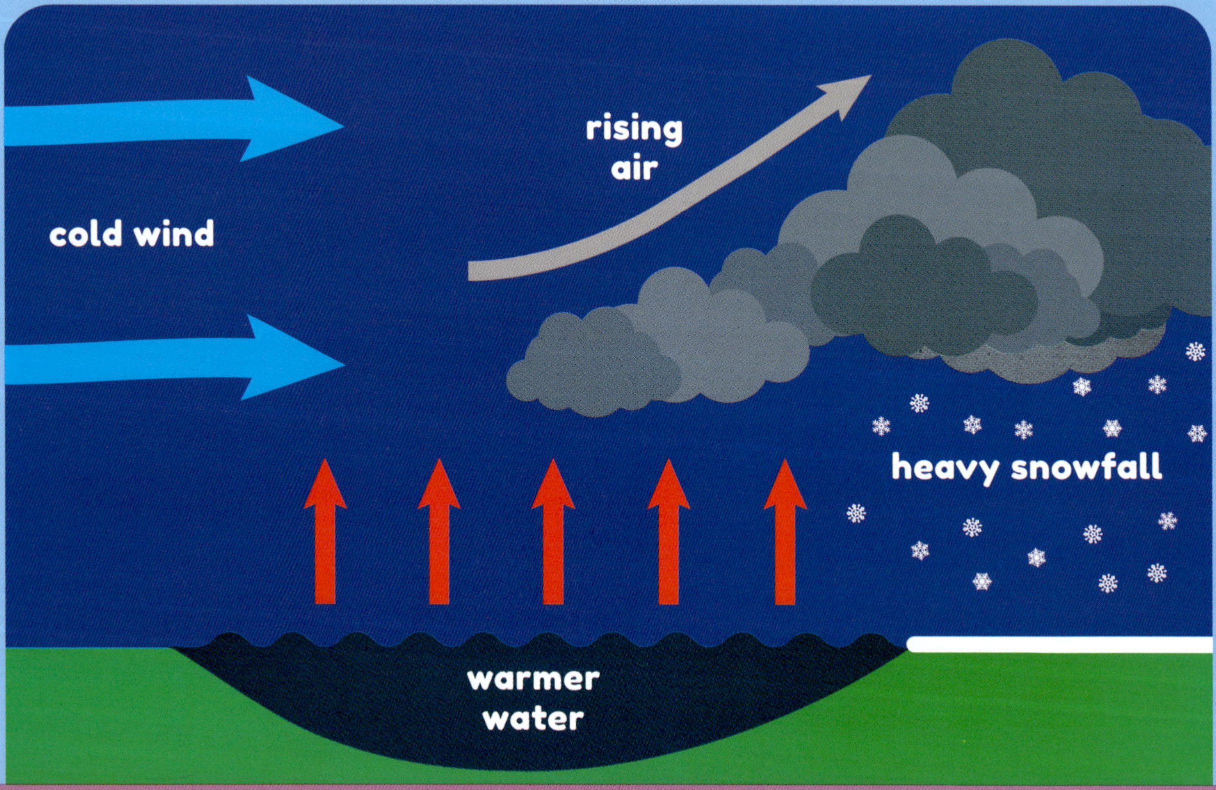

Heavy Snowfall

The moisture falls in heavy bands of snow. This is known as lake-effect snow. It can fall at a rate of three inches (8 cm) per hour or more.

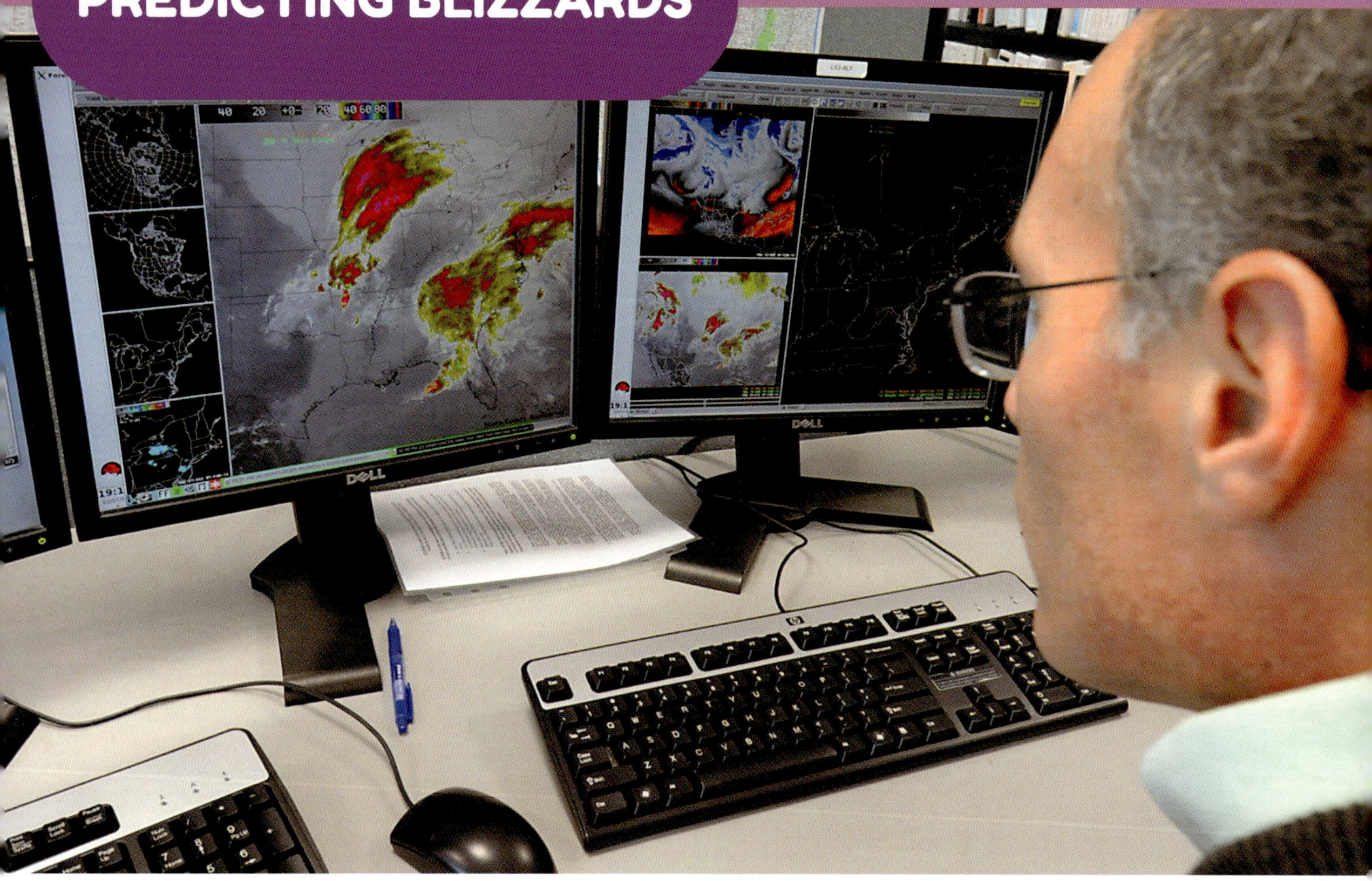

Meteorologists study images and data to make weather forecasts.

Meteorologists

Meteorologists study the weather. Some also forecast the weather. This means they warn people if the weather may get dangerous. They tell people if a blizzard could happen.

A Difficult Job

Meteorologists try to give accurate forecasts. But it is not easy. Winter storms vary in size. Many conditions affect the storms. Conditions can quickly change.

Natural features such as mountains can influence a blizzard.

Satellites

Scientists have many ways to study the weather. One way is with satellites. Satellites are in space. They orbit, or circle, Earth. Some satellites gather information about the weather.

A satellite image shows a large stretch of the US Northeast covered in snow after a 2015 blizzard.

Satellites that study Earth are called environmental satellites.

Current Weather

Earth is always turning. Some satellites move with it. They always stay in the same spot over Earth. The satellites take photos of Earth. The photos can show severe weather such as blizzards.

FUN FACT!

Some satellites over the United States take photos every 15 minutes.

Polar Orbit

A polar satellite's view changes with its orbit and Earth's rotation.

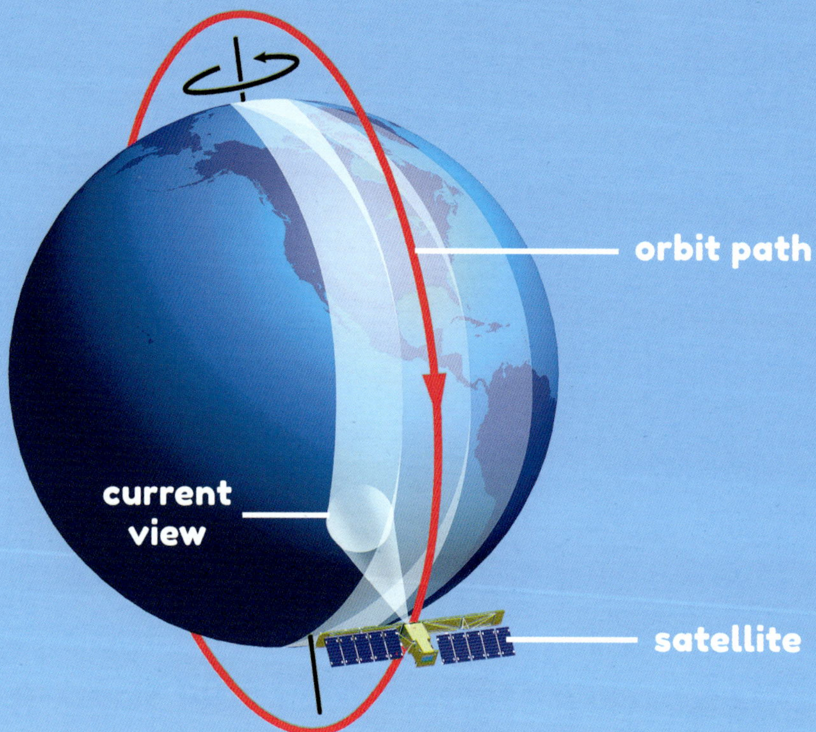

Around Earth

Polar satellites orbit in other directions. They go around Earth's poles. It takes about 1.5 hours to make a full trip.

FUN FACT!

Polar satellites can orbit 518 miles (833 km) above Earth's surface.

Future Weather

Earth rotates under polar satellites. The satellites get a different view with each orbit. In 24 hours, a satellite has gone around 14 times. This gives two full pictures of weather around the world. Scientists look at the images. They use the images to predict the weather.

The Joint Polar Satellite System (JPSS-2) is a polar satellite. It launched in November 2022.

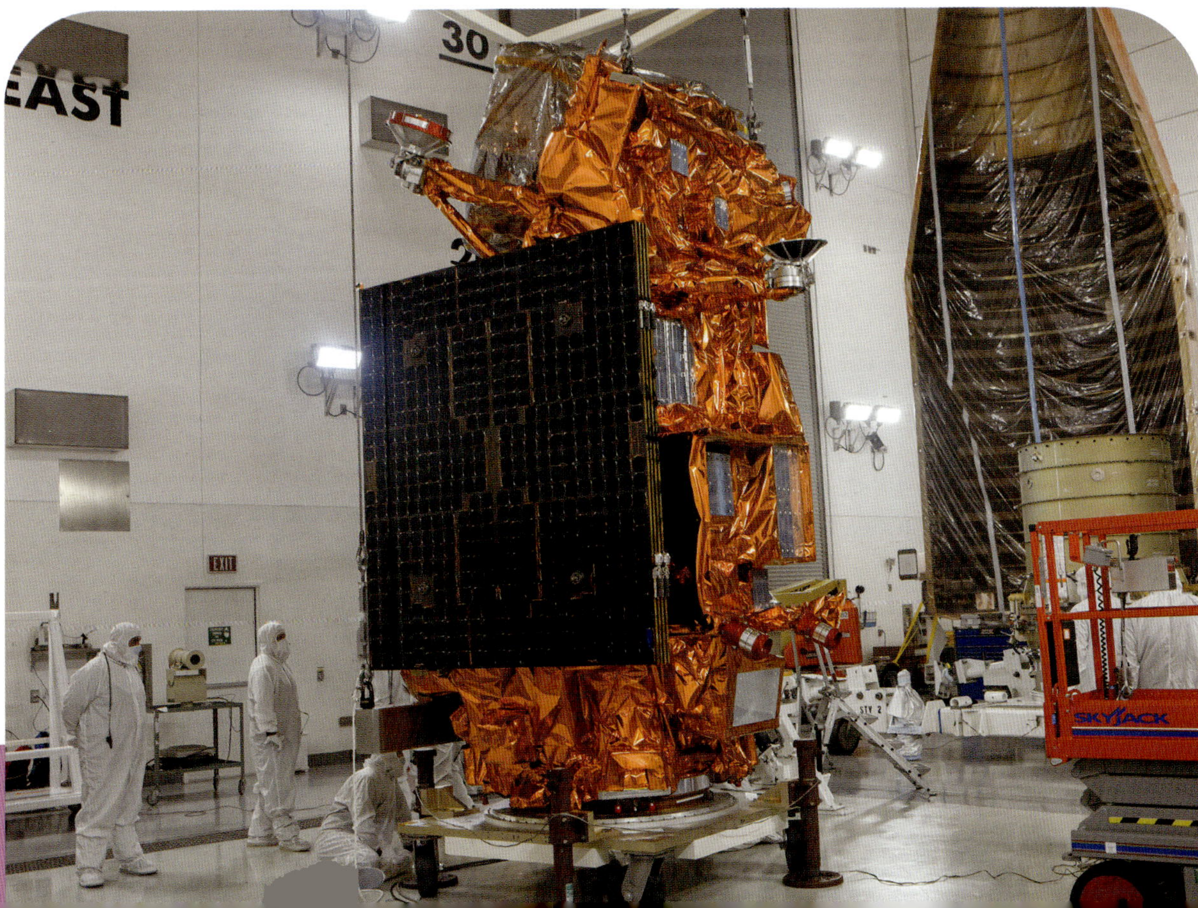

Doppler Radar

Scientists also use Doppler radar. This system helps detect dangerous weather. It is the best way to spot severe storms.

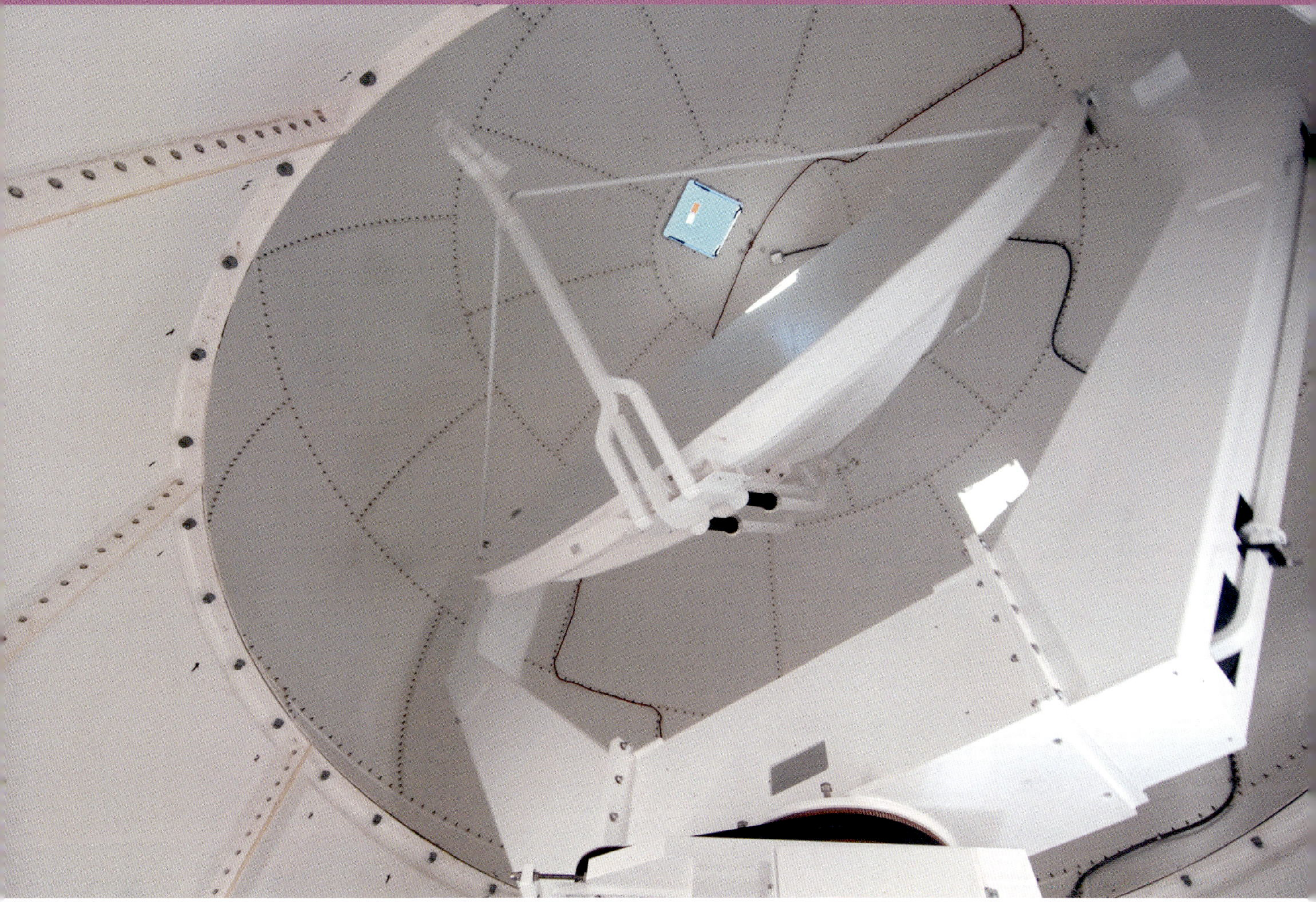

A large dish sits inside the Doppler radar tower's white dome.

Reflected Energy

A radar dish sends out a pulse of energy. The energy hits an object such as a snowflake and scatters. A small amount comes back to the radar.

How Doppler Radar Works

Doppler radar sends pulses at up to 1,300 times a second.

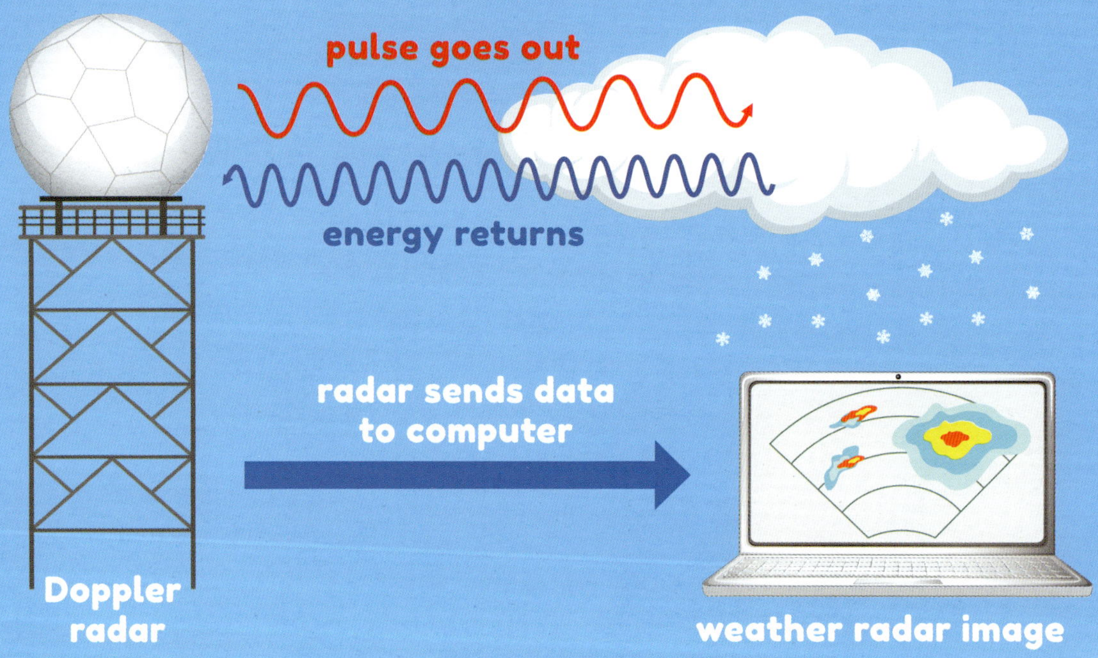

Strength and Time

The radar tracks the way the energy bounces back. It senses the speed of return. It senses the strength of the energy. This information tells how far away precipitation is. It tells whether rain or snow is falling.

Measuring Movement

Doppler radar can tell how fast a storm is moving. It can tell if the storm is moving closer or farther away. It tells wind strength and wind direction.

Radar System

The United States uses the Next Generation Weather Radar system. It is the most advanced radar in the world. It uses 160 Doppler radars.

Computers display a snowstorm's movements based on radar information.

Surface Weather

US scientists also use a program called the Automated Surface Observing System (ASOS). It studies all kinds of weather. It gathers data, or information, near Earth's surface. This includes information about the clouds and temperature. It includes wind direction and wind speed. It also tells types of precipitation.

An anemometer is a tool that ASOS uses to measure wind speed.

Weather Data

ASOS uses many tools to collect data. This information is important for understanding weather patterns. ASOS is always taking in data.

Meteorologists sometimes use portable versions of the same tools used in ASOS to take measurements.

Creating a Forecast

Scientists put all the ASOS data into a computer. The computer estimates what the weather will do next. Scientists check the results. They use their own experience to see if it makes sense. Then they give their forecast.

ASOS and Aircraft

ASOS is important for aircraft. It lets airlines know about weather conditions. That way, they can make safe decisions. Planes can fly in light snow. But they should not take off if a blizzard may happen. Pilots need to see the runway.

Airplanes must wait until a blizzard is over before they can take off.

Weather Balloons

Scientists also check conditions using weather balloons. The balloons use helium or hydrogen to go up into the air. Sensors take measurements in the air.

Researchers in Antarctica inflate a balloon to study the atmosphere.

Researchers need an open space to release weather balloons.

In the Air

The US National Weather Service (NWS) launches weather balloons daily. Some balloons float for more than two hours. They can travel 100 miles (160 km) or more. Weather balloons can reach about 130,000 feet (39,600 m) above sea level.

FUN FACT!

Some people mistake weather balloons for alien spacecraft.

PREDICTING BLIZZARDS

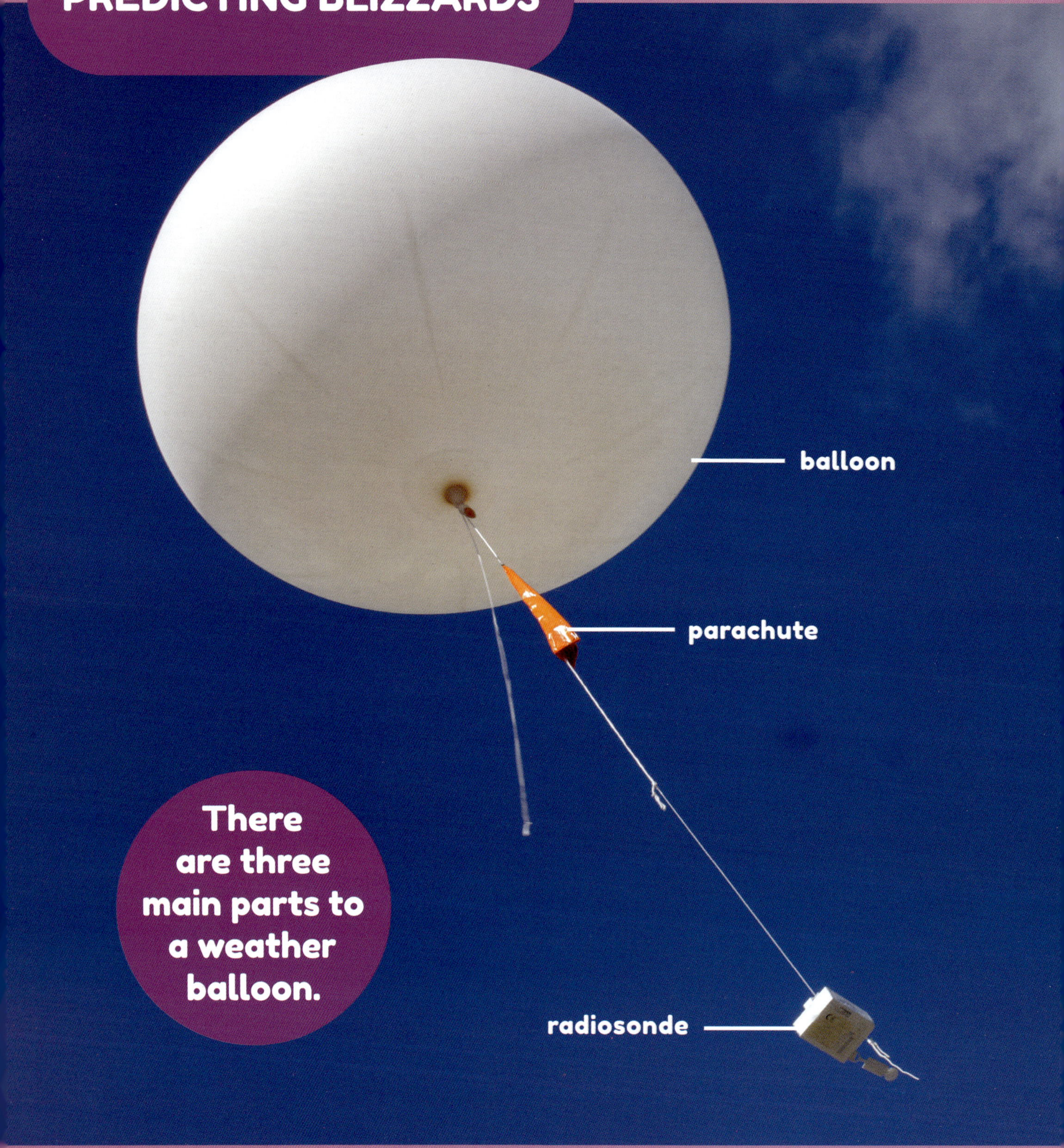

There are three main parts to a weather balloon.

Getting Data

Every weather balloon has a radiosonde. This instrument detects temperature, air pressure, and more. GPS tracks the balloon's path. GPS helps measure the wind speed and wind direction. The radiosonde sends the data back to the scientists.

Back to Earth

Eventually, a weather balloon pops. The radiosonde floats down with a parachute. The balloon, the parachute, and the string can naturally break down. Sometimes people find the radiosondes. These can be reused.

Into a Storm

Scientists launch balloons during blizzards. The radiosonde helps scientists understand the storm. Sometimes, a launch works. Other times, the storm causes the balloon to pop early.

Using the Data

In the United States, the NWS puts data into computers. The computers use the data to help predict the weather. They can predict blizzards.

In 2016, a supercomputer model showed the predicted movement of a December blizzard.

The National Oceanic and Atmospheric Administration (NOAA) runs the NWS. It has supercomputers in Orlando, Florida.

Supercomputers

The computers used are called supercomputers. They are powerful. Information in them is constantly updated.

FUN FACT!

The NWS supercomputers can process information more than 10,000 times faster than many desktop computers.

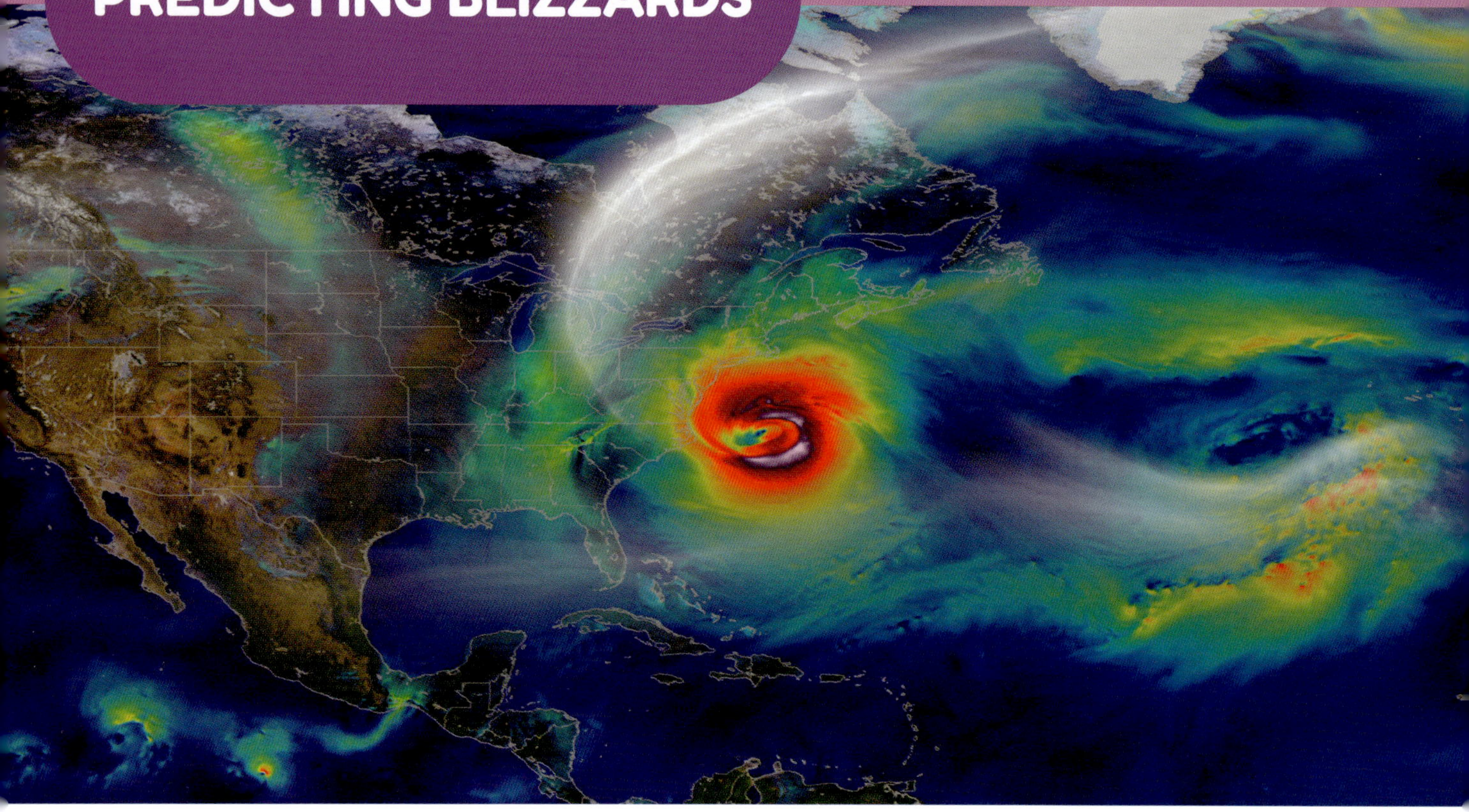

A supercomputer model used data to show the path and the winds of 2012's Hurricane Sandy, which brought snow to northeastern states.

Computer Errors

Supercomputers do not always make the right predictions. A five-day forecast is correct about 90 percent of the time. A seven-day forecast is about 80 percent accurate. A ten-day forecast is right about 50 percent of the time.

Never a Sure Thing

The computers can use only the data they are given. A tiny change in the data can change the result. And some weather systems change more than others. This affects the computer's accuracy.

Supercomputer Sites

The NWS has two main locations with supercomputers. There are two rows of supercomputers at each spot. The rows are 40 feet (12 m) long.

Poor prediction accuracy can make it difficult for people to prepare for a blizzard.

Changes in Moisture

Storms that are several days away are harder to predict. Small details can have a huge effect. For example, the air humidity could change. This affects how much snow an area gets.

Moisture evaporates from lakes at different rates depending on the conditions.

A thermometer shows the temperature.

Changes in Temperature

Temperature also plays a role. It affects the type of snow that falls. As air gets colder, it holds less moisture. The snow is dry. It is easy for the wind to blow. A blizzard is more likely to happen.

Winter Storm Juno brought ice along with blizzard conditions to Massachusetts in January 2015.

Extreme Cold

Blizzards can bring extreme cold. The definition of extreme cold depends on the normal temperatures for the area. It may be any temperature below freezing. Freezing is 32 degrees Fahrenheit (0°C).

Danger to People

Extreme cold is dangerous for people. The body keeps a constant temperature. In extreme cold, it must work hard to keep warm. It may not be able to heat up enough.

Extreme cold is most dangerous to children and elderly people. They lose body heat faster than the average adult.

Wind and Temperature

Blizzard winds make extreme cold even more dangerous. Cold winds carry heat away from the body. Stronger winds carry heat away faster than slower winds. The body's temperature goes down very quickly.

Warm clothes help protect the body from cold wind.

Windchill affects people and other animals. But it does not affect plants.

Windchill

Wind makes the temperature feel colder than it is. This effect is called windchill. Windchill is how cold the current temperature would feel without wind. For example, a windy day that's 20 degrees Fahrenheit (–7°C) might feel like ten degrees Fahrenheit (–12°C). The windchill is ten degrees Fahrenheit (–12°C).

FUN FACT!

The coldest US windchill ever recorded was –108 degrees Fahrenheit (–78°C). It happened in New Hampshire in 2023.

Frostbite Stages

The fingers are among the body parts most at risk of frostbite.

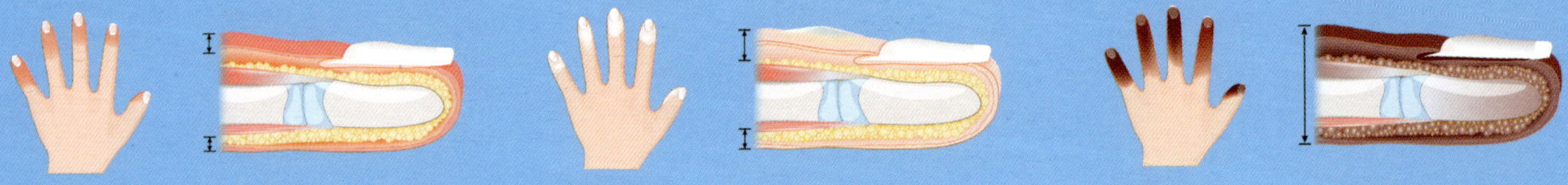

1. FROSTNIP
Symptoms: Pain, tingling, numbness, red or purple skin. Does not cause permanent damage.

Affected area

2. SUPERFICIAL FROSTBITE
Symptoms: Skin feels warm, pins and needles feeling. Skin may blister or turn blotchy when warmed up. Seek medical attention.

3. DEEP FROSTBITE
Symptoms: Lower layers of skin freeze. Area feels totally numb and is difficult to move. After warming up, blisters form and the skin turns black. Seek medical attention.

Frostbite

Cold temperatures can put people at risk of frostbite. This is when cold temperatures damage the skin. Sometimes, the damage cannot heal. A windchill of –20 degrees Fahrenheit (–29°C) can cause frostbite in 30 minutes.

Hypothermia

Cold temperatures can also cause hypothermia. This is when the body loses heat faster than it can produce it. The body's temperature gets too low. The body stops working normally. If not treated, the person can die.

Symptoms of hypothermia include shivering, confusion, and drowsiness.

Heavy Snowfall

Blizzards can bring large amounts of snow. Heavy snow can knock over power lines. This causes power outages. Without electricity, people may not be able to heat their homes. Pipes can freeze. Then people do not have access to water.

Strong winds and heavy snow can cause trees to fall on power lines.

Even large buildings' roofs can collapse under very heavy snow.

Collapsing Roofs

Roofs can support normal amounts of snow. But in a blizzard, a lot of snow can pile up. The snow is very heavy. It can cause roofs to cave in.

It can be hard to tell how deep snowdrifts are.

Drifting Snow

During a blizzard, some snow stays close to the ground. This is called drifting snow. It does not limit visibility as much as blowing snow does. Sometimes wind blows the snow in the same direction for several hours. It forms large piles. These are called snowdrifts.

Snowed In

Snowdrifts can pile up several feet deep. They form against homes and other buildings. They can block windows and doors. People may not be able to get out.

FUN FACT!

One of the highest snowdrifts was recorded in 1888. It was 52 feet (16 m) tall.

Snowdrifts may almost entirely cover small buildings.

Driving

Drifting snow is dangerous for drivers. This is especially true when the sun is shining. It reflects off the snow. This makes it hard to see the road. Snowdrifts can also make the roads icy.

When many cars drive over snow on a road, the snow packs together. Packed snow can cause tires to slip.

People in Washington, DC, had to walk in order to get groceries when a blizzard struck in 2016.

Blocking Roads

Snowdrifts may also block the roads. It can be hard for trucks to deliver food, gasoline, and other supplies. Emergency workers may not be able to reach people. People may not be able to get the help they need.

Slick roads can cause vehicles to slide into ditches or ponds.

Dangerous Travel

Heavy snow and snowdrifts make it difficult to travel by car. Roads may be closed. Traveling even a short distance is dangerous. Cars may slide on ice or snow. Many car accidents happen.

Stranded on the Roads

Cars often get stuck in the snow. People may become stranded in their cars. They could have to wait for hours before help arrives.

People may try to push cars that get stuck in snow.

Cutting Off Communication

When power lines fall, communication systems often go down. This includes phone and internet services. People may be unable to contact family members or emergency workers.

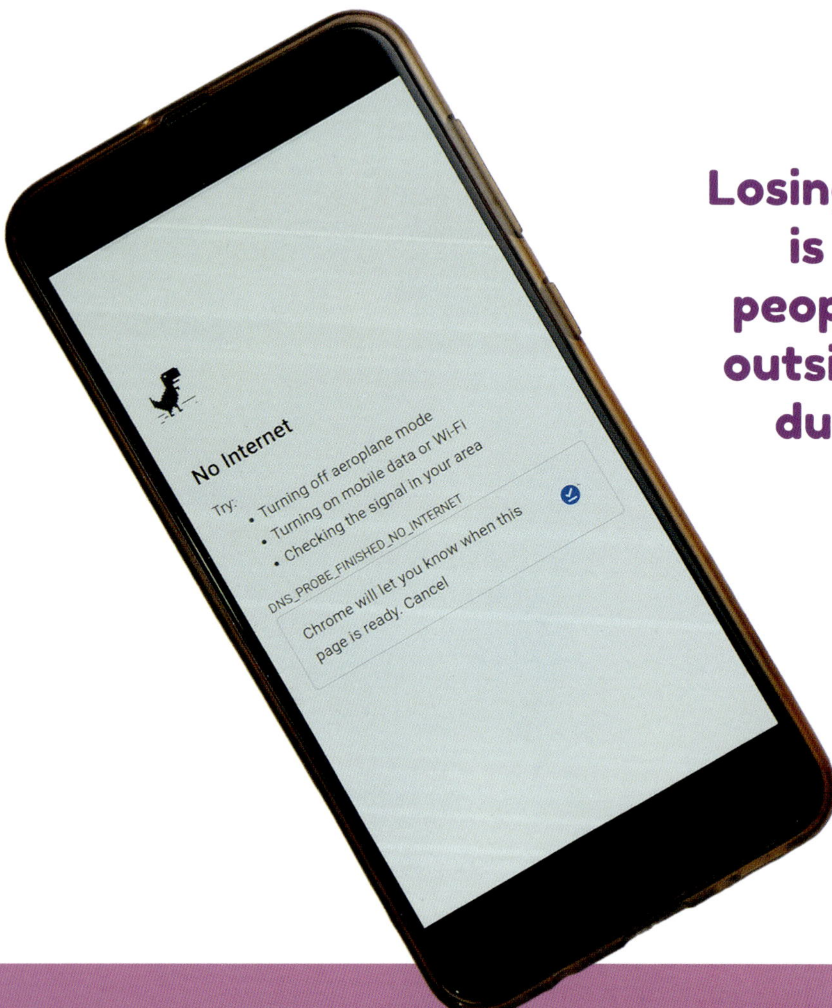

Losing communications is dangerous for people who are stuck outside or in a vehicle during a blizzard.

Grocery store shelves may be nearly empty of essential food and bottled water as people prepare for a blizzard.

Bringing Everything to a Halt

A blizzard affects the whole community. Road conditions make it too dangerous for students to go to school. People cannot go to the store or work. Airports close. Blizzards can make it impossible to travel in entire cities or regions.

STAYING SAFE FROM BLIZZARDS

People check weather apps to find out if a blizzard is expected in their area.

Warning Systems

A warning system tells if a blizzard may be coming. Emergency alerts help people plan. In the United States, the NWS sends the alerts.

Blizzard Watch

A blizzard watch is the first alert. It means the area may get a blizzard within the next few days. There is a 50 percent chance a blizzard could happen. Scientists are not sure of the location or time. They are not sure how severe it will be.

A blizzard watch gives people time to prepare if a blizzard does come.

Advisory

A winter weather advisory means snow, freezing rain, or sleet is starting to collect. Snow could reach three to five inches (8 to 13 cm) in 12 hours. Sleet can be up to 0.5 inches (1.3 cm).

Freezing rain can combine with sleet or snow during an advisory. This makes roads and sidewalks slick.

Blizzard Warning System

The NWS has winter weather notices that indicate the likelihood of a blizzard.

BLIZZARD WATCH

Conditions could lead to a blizzard.

WINTER WEATHER ADVISORY

One or more of the following is possible:

- Three to five inches (8 to 13 cm) of snow in 12 hours
- More than 0.5 inches (1.3 cm) of sleet
- Freezing rain with sleet or snow
- Blowing snow

BLIZZARD WARNING

Blizzard conditions expected for at least three hours

Warnings

Blizzard warnings come when a blizzard will probably happen. There must be an 80 percent chance or more in the next 36 hours. The conditions could be life threatening.

A wood-burning fireplace can help heat a home without using electricity.

Staying Warm

It's important to prepare for a blizzard. People need a way to stay warm if the power goes out. They will need extra winter clothing and blankets. They should have an emergency source of heat. This could be a fireplace or a small stove.

Emergency Kits

People should also make an emergency kit. The kit should include a flashlight or lantern and extra batteries. Some radios use a hand crank or batteries. These radios keep people updated on the storm if there is no power or cell service.

Weather radios may have a flashlight built in.

Food and Water

People may not be able to go anywhere for several days. The emergency kit should have enough water and food for each person. It should be enough for at least three days. The food should not need to be refrigerated or cooked.

Protein bars are among the food items often included in an emergency kit.

The American Red Cross website includes a list of items to keep in a first aid kit.

First Aid

The emergency kit should also have first aid supplies. This includes any medications needed. It can also include an emergency whistle. People can blow the whistle to signal for help.

Having a physical copy of emergency contacts can be helpful if the power goes out and a phone cannot be charged.

Communication Plan

It is important to have a plan to stay in contact during a blizzard. Family members should decide where to meet if they get separated. Everyone in the family should have a list of emergency contacts.

Checking on Neighbors

People may have elderly neighbors. Or a neighbor may have been ill. People should check on these neighbors to make sure they are safe. If they cannot call, they should go to the neighbor's home. They can make sure the neighbor has food and heat.

People can shovel sidewalks and driveways for neighbors who cannot clear snow themselves.

Providing for Pets

Pets also need food, water, and blankets. Dogs should be kept on a leash when outside. That way, they will not get lost. Old dogs and puppies are more at risk of hypothermia. So are dogs with short, thin fur. They will stay warmer with a coat or sweater.

Each dog's cold tolerance is unique. Owners should watch for signs a dog is cold, including shivering and curling up tight in warm spots.

An ID tag can include information such as the owner's phone number.

Pet IDs

Owners should make sure their pets have identification. This can be a collar with tags. It can be a microchip. Pets can get lost in a blizzard. If someone finds a pet, an ID will help them find its home.

Livestock should have free access to their shelter during blizzards.

Shelter

Livestock also need protection during a blizzard. They should have a sturdy shelter. It should be able to stand up against high winds. Livestock also need warm bedding.

Food and Water

Animals should have enough food and water for a couple of days. They need enough in case people are not able to reach them right away. If the temperatures are extremely cold, the water will freeze. Someone will need to break the ice so the animals can drink.

The average adult horse needs to eat between 24 and 30 pounds (11 and 14 kg) of hay each day during winter.

Preparing the Home

Before winter begins, people can prepare their homes. This way, they will be ready if a blizzard comes. They will need a safe source of heat. But there are also things they can do to help keep out the cold.

Preparing a home for a blizzard can be important for staying safe in the storm.

Insulation keeps warm air inside the home from escaping outside.

Insulation

Homes should have enough insulation. Insulation is material used under the floors, in the walls, and in attics. It creates a barrier between the inside of the home and the freezing temperatures outside.

Protecting the Pipes

It's important to insulate pipes in garages, in attics, and under houses. This helps keep the water in the pipes from freezing. Frozen pipes can burst. This can flood the house.

Caulk can seal gaps around windows.

Caulk

People should also seal any cracks or openings in their homes. Otherwise, the cold air can get inside. Caulk is a flexible material that can seal gaps. It is waterproof. It will not be affected by the snow.

Weather Strips

Weather strips are strips of material used to help seal a house. They can be plastic, metal, or foam. Weather-stripping seals air leaks around things that open, such as doors and windows.

Weather-stripping closes gaps between a door and its frame.

No Visibility

Sometimes people cannot get home before a blizzard comes. They should drive very slowly. If it is too hard to see, they should pull over to the side. They should stay in their cars and wait for the storm to end.

Driving slowly during a blizzard helps prevent crashes.

Stuck in the Snow

Sometimes cars get stuck in the snow. People should stay in their cars. It is colder outside than in a car. Also, they can still get some heat in their cars. They can turn on their cars for about ten minutes every hour.

A car's exhaust pipe is close to the ground. Snow can cover it.

Avoiding Carbon Monoxide

Carbon monoxide is a poisonous gas. It comes from a car's exhaust pipe when the car is running. It can leak into the car. People should open a window a little to get fresh air.

A Clear Exhaust Pipe

Sometimes snow gathers in the car's exhaust pipe. It can block the pipe. Then the carbon monoxide goes into the car. People can get out to remove the snow from the pipe. But then they should get back inside and wait.

A blizzard can bury a car in snow. It's important to clear snow away before running the car.

Going Outdoors

People should stay indoors during a blizzard. If they must go out, they should dress warmly. They should wear many layers of clothing. Water-repellent coats and jackets help people stay dry.

Warm winter clothing helps keep people from freezing if they have to go out in a blizzard.

Protecting the Body

Extremely cold air can hurt the lungs. People with lung diseases must be especially careful. They should cover their

nose and mouth when outside. The cold can also put extra strain on the heart. People with heart problems should avoid physical activities in a blizzard.

Gloves or Mittens?

Mittens are warmer than gloves. Fingers can share warmth in mittens. And there is less surface area for heat to escape.

If a large amount of snow melts quickly, it can cause flooding.

After the Storm

People must still be careful after a blizzard is over. Melting snow can cause floods. Creeks and rivers may overflow. If people think their home might flood, they should leave until the risk is over.

Icy Roads

People should listen for updates on road conditions. Plows clear snow from roads after a blizzard. But roads still may not be safe for driving. Water left on the roads can freeze. This creates a clear sheet of ice called black ice. Cars can slide on the ice.

Snowplows drop salt or other substances onto roads to help ice melt.

Clearing the Roofs

After a blizzard, people may want to clear their roofs of snow. They may use a roof snow rake. The rake has a long handle. People can reach the roof from the ground. Then they can pull the snow off the roof.

Snow rakes help people remove snow from the edges of their roofs.

Large icicles that fall can give a person a concussion or other injuries.

Falling Ice and Snow

People must be careful when raking their roofs. Ice or snow can fall in large pieces. It is very heavy. It can damage things below it. It can hurt someone standing below.

Power plants burn fossil fuels to produce electricity.

Climate Change

Climate change refers to changes in weather patterns. It is caused by certain human activities. These include burning fuels such as natural gas, coal, and oil. This produces large amounts of a gas called carbon dioxide. Carbon dioxide traps some heat in the atmosphere. Heat is important for life on Earth. But too much carbon dioxide can cause temperatures to get too hot.

The Snow Continues

Warmer temperatures could lead to fewer blizzards. There are fewer places that experience extremely cold temperatures than in the past. But some areas still get snow. Blizzards have become more severe in those places.

New York City has been getting less snow than it has historically gotten. But it still snows sometimes.

Extra Moisture

Many scientists think climate change could make blizzards more intense. This is because warmer air holds more moisture. The moisture will eventually become precipitation. If the temperature is cold enough, it becomes snow. If the wind is fast enough, the extra moisture could create stronger storms.

Large amounts of heavy snow weigh down tree branches.

In December 2017, the Buffalo Bills and Indianapolis Colts played during a lake-effect snowstorm.

Big Storms

Some scientists believe that climate change will make winters shorter. But there will still be times when it is cold enough for snow. During that time, the moisture in the air will create huge snowstorms.

On the Rise

Temperature is measured in degrees. For each degree Fahrenheit (0.6°C) it goes up, the air holds about 4 percent more water.

BLIZZARDS AND CLIMATE CHANGE

More evaporation of ocean water forms more clouds.

Warmer Oceans

Oceans cover about 70 percent of Earth's surface. Changes in the climate affect the oceans. As temperatures rise, the oceans absorb more heat. The surface temperatures of the oceans rise.

More Moisture

The warmer ocean temperatures cause more water to evaporate. This means there is more moisture in the atmosphere over the ocean. There is more moisture available to storms. This can make a storm more severe.

FUN FACT!

Oceans absorb more than 90 percent of the extra heat produced by human activities.

Storms that start over the ocean can move to colder areas.

Melting Snow and Ice

Climate change affects the cold Arctic regions. These regions are also warming. The snow and ice melt faster. The melting snow and ice make the sea levels rise.

Melting Arctic ice causes polar bear habitat to shrink.

A winter storm brought heavy wind and snow to the US Northeast on January 9, 2024.

The US Northeast

The warmer temperatures and melting ice can change wind patterns in the Arctic. This allows cold Arctic air to move into the United States. The cold air could cause more high-pressure systems to form in the North Atlantic. Cold storms move more slowly than warmer ones. The storms last longer and become more intense.

In 2022, Hamburg, New York, received five feet (1.5 m) of snow from a November storm.

Warmer Water, More Snow

Climate change could also cause changes in lake-effect snow. It may cause more or less snow than usual. For example, climate change can cause water temperatures to rise. Ice may not form as quickly on the lakes. More moisture goes into the air. This can create more snow during a blizzard.

Warmer Temperatures, Less Snow

But climate change may also cause less snow. The temperatures may become too warm for snow. Instead of snow, rain falls instead.

Climate change could cause some places to get more rain and less snow in winter.

Famous Blizzard

One of the most famous blizzards happened in March 1888 in the United States. On March 10, temperatures in the Northeast were about 55 degrees Fahrenheit (13°C). In the middle of the country, a low-pressure system stretched from Canada to the Gulf of Mexico. It moved quickly east.

New York City did not have a well-organized street cleaning system in 1888. Children helped clear snow.

Two Storms

The system had two storms. A southern storm brought rain. A northern storm brought snow. By evening, the northern storm was becoming weaker. The southern storm was moving out to sea from the Carolinas.

In 1888, the US Signal Service tracked weather. It was part of the War Department.

A Sudden Change

The official forecast for the Northeast for March 11 was fair weather. Rain would come in the evening. But the southern storm turned north. It pulled in water from the ocean. The storm turned west and made a loop over New York. Temperatures dropped.

No More Fair Weather

Cold Arctic air came from Canada. It mixed with moist air. Rain changed to hail. Then the hail changed to sleet. Just after midnight, it changed to snow. Wind gusts were 80 miles per hour (129 kmh).

Strong winds blew snow through New York City.

New York City

The morning of March 12 saw a complete whiteout in New York City. In some areas, snow was 40 to 50 inches (102 to 127 cm) deep. Snowdrifts reached between 30 and 40 feet (9 and 12 m) deep. Communication wires were down. There was no way to send messages.

Parts of New York City had masses of overhead wires. Snow and wind could damage them.

Trolleys, which ran along streets on tracks, got stuck in the snow.

Trapped on Trains

Without communication wires, people could not get weather updates. Many city residents went to work even in the snow. They rode on trains. But snowdrifts blocked many trains for at least two days. Up to 15,000 passengers were stranded. The snow also caused train accidents across the Northeast.

Finding Fuel

Passenger cars on the trains had woodstoves for warmth. But the wood ran out. People chopped up tables and seats to use as fuel. Many travelers tried to walk home.

GREAT BLIZZARD, USA, 1888

Artists have made engravings showing New Yorkers during the Great Blizzard.

A Deadly Storm

The blizzard finally ended on March 14. It went from Maryland to Maine. The storm killed more than 400 people. Of those, about 200 were from New York City. Some died from accidents. Some froze in the cold. Others were unable to get food or medical help. Thousands of animals also froze in the blizzard.

Making Changes

In New York City, trains, communication lines, water lines, and gas lines had been built above ground. But the wind and ice from the storm destroyed many of them. After the storm, officials moved them underground. They started building an underground subway system within ten years.

Widespread

The storm was also severe on Long Island and in Albany, New York, as well as New Jersey and Connecticut. The blizzard stranded about 50 trains outside New York City.

New York City's subway system has 665 miles (1,070 km) of tracks.

Brewing Storm

On March 7, 1993, computer models predicted an intense low-pressure system. It was forming over the Gulf of Mexico. Scientists began giving warnings about the storm.

The 1993 North American Storm Complex is also called the Storm of the Century.

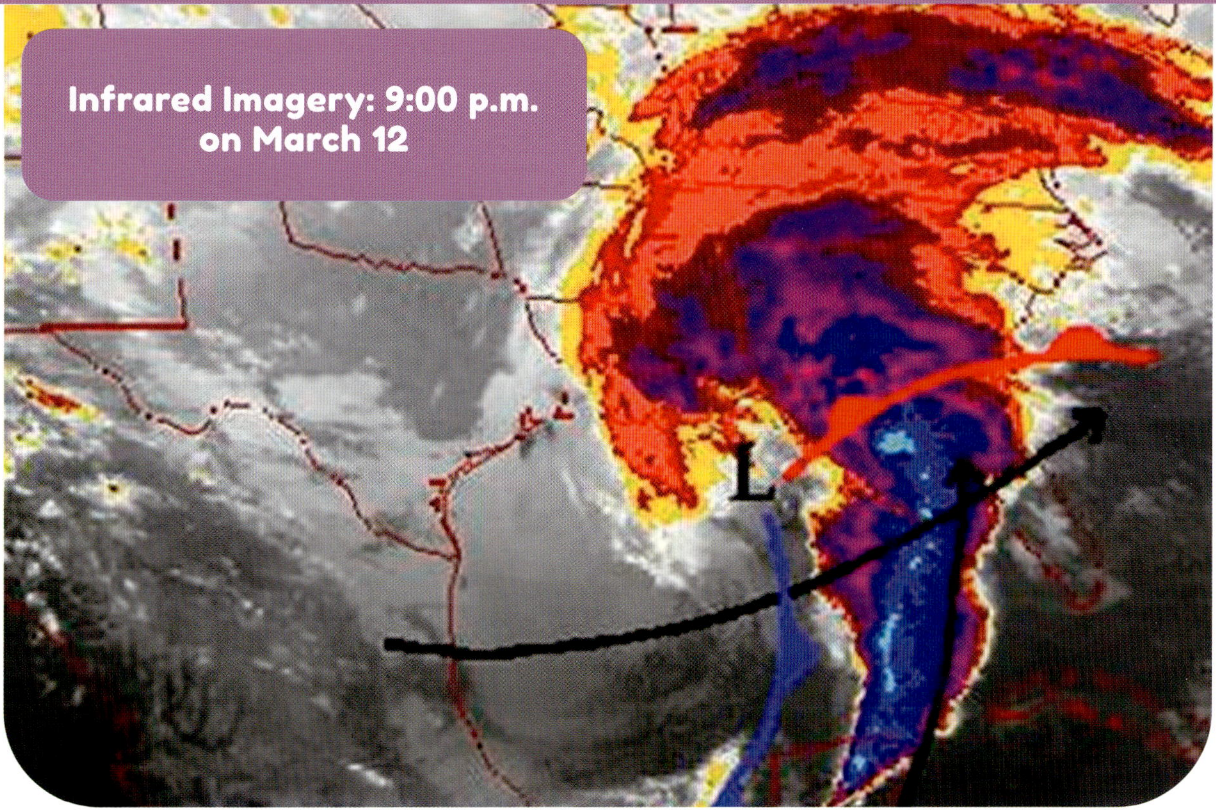

An infrared image from 1993 shows the development of the storm.

Growing in the Gulf

On March 12, the low-pressure system was near the coast of Texas. Strong winds developed across the eastern United States. This helped the system grow. Storms on the coast added more energy. The system moved across the Gulf of Mexico to Florida.

Thunderstorms and Tornadoes

On March 13, severe thunderstorms caused strong winds and tornadoes in Florida. That day, the low-pressure system moved across Georgia. It met cold air coming from the north. This made snow and blizzards in the South.

FUN FACT!

Up to six inches (15 cm) of snow fell in parts of northern Florida.

Winds and Snow

The low-pressure system continued to grow. During the height of the storm, two to three inches (5 to 8 cm) of snow fell per hour. Some areas got up to 60 inches (152 cm) of snow. Wind gusts blew at more than 100 miles per hour (160 kmh).

Snow Totals

The storm caused snow to fall across a large stretch of the United States.

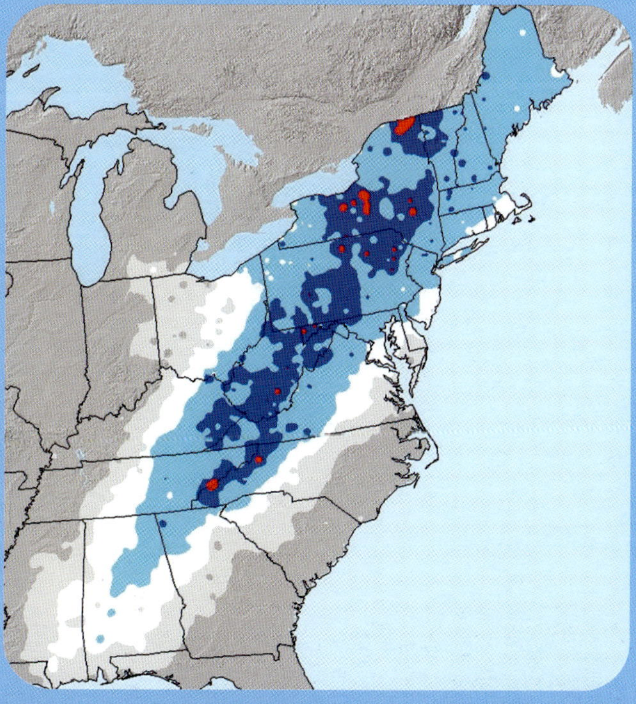

Blocking Roads

The snow blocked the roads for thousands of people. People in the mountains got the most snow. More than 200 hikers needed rescue in the Tennessee and North Carolina mountains.

People had to dig out their cars from under the snow in Maine.

Massachusetts governor William Weld gave updates about the emergency on March 14.

Deadly Conditions

Some people died from being caught in the snow. The storm also caused flooding in coastal states. People in those states died from drowning. Tornadoes killed others. More than 270 people in 13 states died in all.

LaGuardia Airport in New York was one of many that closed due to heavy snowfall.

Other Effects

The storm lasted for three days. It was over by March 15. It directly affected about 40 percent of the US population. About ten million people lost power. The storm closed every major US airport on the East Coast at some point while it moved across the area.

An Accurate Forecast

FUN FACT!

The storm moved at 70 miles per hour (113 kmh) at one point.

The storm became an important turning point in predictions. The forecasts came days ahead of the storm. The early warnings likely saved many lives. But some people still did not understand how dangerous the storm could be. Officials tried to find better ways to predict threats. They improved their forecast accuracy.

In Albany, New York, dump trucks brought snow cleared from the storm to a river.

Mountain Snow

Afghanistan is a country in southern Asia. Most of the country has a dry climate. Two mountain ranges run through the center. A lot of snow falls in the mountains during the winter.

Afghanistan summers are very hot. Some areas can reach more than 122 degrees Fahrenheit (50°C).

Snow Brings Water

Many people live in the valleys between the mountains. Warm weather melts the snow. It provides water for crops during the dry summer.

AFGHANISTAN BLIZZARD, 2008

Mud huts may use tarps to help keep out water.

Living Conditions

The mountain villages are often remote. Most people live in homes made of mud and straw. People travel mainly by foot.

A Blizzard Blows In

In 2008, Afghanistan experienced one of its worst winters. Heavy snow fell in January. In February, a blizzard covered part of the country in blinding snow.

Winter usually lasts from December through February in Afghanistan.

Lost in the Snow

During the storm, temperatures dropped to –22 degrees Fahrenheit (–30°C). Nearly six feet (2 m) of snow fell. Many people were caught in the storm. Some took days to find their way home. Others did not survive.

The winter of 2007–2008 was considered the worst in Afghanistan in 30 years.

Trucks with supplies struggled to travel through snow and mud.

Cut Off

The storm destroyed more than 800 houses. Some people died when their roofs caved in. The mountain villages were cut off from larger cities. Government workers, military troops, and other groups tried to help. But it was hard to reach the people.

People gathered wood to burn for warmth.

Dangerous Cold

People caught in the blizzard began walking to towns to get help. As they did, many got frostbite. The frostbite was serious in some. They needed fingers, hands, toes, or feet removed.

Many Lives Lost

The 2008 Afghanistan Blizzard was part of a very deadly winter. The snow and cold killed

926 people. More than 316,000 livestock animals died. Many people who survived had lost their main source of income.

Many of the livestock had no shelter from the storm.

GLOSSARY

accurate
Correct or close to the truth or standard.

air pressure
The pressing weight of air on a surface as gravity pulls the air toward Earth.

conditions
The circumstances such as temperature, wind speed, and more that make up weather.

evaporate
To change from a liquid such as water into vapor in the air.

exhaust pipe
A pipe through which waste gases are released from an engine.

forecast
A prediction of future weather.

GPS
Global Positioning System, a system that uses satellites to find a location on Earth.

gust
A sudden, strong blast of wind.

humidity
The degree of moisture in the air.

microchip
A small electronic chip with a unique number for identification that is placed under an animal's skin.

musket
A type of firearm with a long barrel that was used in the past.

precipitation
Rain, snow, and other forms of moisture that fall from the sky.

TO LEARN MORE

More Books to Read

Buckey, A. W. *Weather*. Abdo, 2025.

Korté, Steve. *What Was the Children's Blizzard of 1888?* Penguin Workshop, 2023.

Weather. DK, 2022.

Online Resources

Booklinks
NONFICTION NETWORK
FREE! ONLINE NONFICTION RESOURCES

To learn more about blizzards, please visit **abdobooklinks.com** or scan this QR code. These links are routinely monitored and updated to provide the most current information available.

INDEX

PHOTO CREDITS

Cover Photos: Shutterstock Images, front (girl), back (icicles, sign); Robert Wiik/Shutterstock Images, front (plow)

Interior Photos: Alexey Kljatov/Shutterstock Images, 1; Alexey Vanin/Shutterstock Images, 3; Shutterstock Images, 4, 5 (top), 5 (bottom), 7 (top left, top right), 7 (bottom left), 7 (bottom right), 8, 10, 11 (top), 11 (bottom), 15 (top), 15 (bottom), 17 (top), 25, 32, 33 (top), 41, 45 (top), 46, 50, 52, 55, 64, 66, 70, 71, 72, 77, 79 (top), 79 (bottom), 80, 81, 82, 87 (bottom), 94, 95 (bottom), 97, 107 (bottom), 109 (top), 112; Mats Andersson/TT News Agency/AFP/Getty Images, 6; Red Line Editorial, 9 (clouds, background, rain), 9 (snow), 21, 22 (background, clouds), 22 (snow), 67; Robert Gauthier/Los Angeles Times/Getty Images, 12; Alan & Sandy Carey/Science Source, 13; Phil Woolley/Shutterstock Images, 14; Jeff Swensen/Getty Images News/Getty Images, 16; Jonathan Nackstrand/AFP/Getty Images, 17 (bottom); Scott Eisen/Getty Images News/Getty Images, 18; Kevin Dietsch/Getty Images News/Getty Images, 19; Ann Cantelow/Shutterstock Images, 20–21; John Normile/Getty Images News/Getty Images, 23, 100; Lori Van Buren/Albany Times Union/Hearst Newspapers/Getty Images, 24; NOAA/NASA, 26; NASA, 27, 38, 42, 44; QA International/Science Source, 28; Carlos R. V./NASA, 29; Steven Bourelle/Shutterstock Images, 30; Troy Cryder/NASA, 31; John Tlumacki/Boston Globe/Getty Images, 33 (bottom); Wattanasit Chunopas/Shutterstock Images, 34; iStockphoto, 35; Jane Barlow/PA Images/Getty Images, 36; Tom Demerly/US Air National Guard/DVIDS, 37; Carla Thomas/NASA, 39; Kim Shiflett/NASA, 40; NOAA, 43, 59; Andrew Caballero-Reynolds/AFP/Getty Images, 45 (bottom); Natali Sam/Shutterstock Images, 47; Staff Sgt. Steven C. Eaton/Massachusetts National Guard/DVIDS, 48; Brendan Smialowski/AFP/Getty Images, 49; Misa Razdikova/Shutterstock Images, 51; Goran Pehrson/Shutterstock Images, 53; Gregory Rec/Portland Press Herald/Getty Images, 54; Yuriy Brykaylo/Shutterstock Images, 56; Al Geba/Shutterstock Images, 57; Igumnova Irina/Shutterstock Images, 58; Shawn Patrick Ouellette/Portland Press Herald/Getty Images, 60; Mariia Masich/Shutterstock Images, 61; Najmi Arif/Shutterstock Images, 62; Nicholas Kamm/AFP/Getty Images, 63; Joe Raedle/Getty Images News/Getty Images, 65; Alena Ozerova/Shutterstock Images, 68; Guy J. Sagi/Shutterstock Images, 69; Branislav Nenin/Shutterstock Images, 73; Kerem Yucel/AFP/Getty Images, 74; Eric Isselee/Shutterstock Images, 75; Andrew Cline/Shutterstock Images, 76; Tayfun Coskun/Anadolu/Getty Images, 78; Mario Tama/Getty Images News/Getty Images, 83; Rungsan Sununta/Shutterstock Images, 84; Andrew Theodorakis/Getty Images News/Getty Images, 85; Tatiana Buzmakova/Shutterstock Images, 86; Peter Pike/Shutterstock Images, 87 (top); Sgt. Darius Brown/Massachusetts National Guard/DVIDS, 88; Miro Vrlik Photography/Shutterstock Images, 89; Maria Dryfhout/Shutterstock Images, 90; Olga Solo/Shutterstock Images, 91; Kena Betancur/VIEWpress/Corbis News/Getty Images, 92; Maya K. Photography/Shutterstock Images, 93; Brett Carlsen/Getty Images Sport/Getty Images, 95 (top); EB Adventure Photography/Shutterstock Images, 96; Vladimir Turkenich/Shutterstock Images, 98; Lauren Dauphin/NASA, 99; John A. Anderson/Shutterstock Images, 101; Bettmann Archive/Getty Images, 102; Michael Tatman/Shutterstock Images, 103; H. A. Ogden/Library of Congress, 104; C. H. Jordan & Co./Library of Congress, 105; FLHC 3/Alamy, 106; Bettmann/Getty Images, 107 (top); DEA/ICAS94/De Agostini/Getty Images, 108; Leonard Zhukovsky/Shutterstock Images, 109 (bottom); Robert Clark/AP Images, 110, NWS/NOAA, 111, 113; David A. Rogers/Portland Press Herald/Getty Images, 114; George Rizer/Boston Globe/Getty Images, 115; William McGinn/AP Images, 116; Skip Dickstein/Albany Times Union/Hearst Newspapers/Getty Images, 117; Nasir Ahmad Salehi/Shutterstock Images, 118; Massoud Hossaini/AFP/Getty Images, 119, 121; Qais Usyan/AFP/Getty Images, 120; Mark Pearson, 122, 123, 124, 125